# SPIRIT AND FLIGHT

# SPIRIT AND FLIGHT

## A PHOTOGRAPHIC SALUTE
## TO THE
## UNITED STATES AIR FORCE ACADEMY

### PHOTOGRAPHY AND DESIGN BY
### ELIZABETH GILL LUI

FOREWORD BY
BRIGADIER GENERAL MALHAM M. WAKIN, USAF (RETIRED)

RECOLLECTIONS BY
WALTER A. NETSCH, F.A.I.A.

ASSOCIATION OF GRADUATES
UNITED STATES AIR FORCE ACADEMY
*PUBLISHER*

First Published in the United States of America, 1996
by the
Association of Graduates, United States Air Force Academy
3116 Academy Drive
USAFA, Colorado 80840-4475

Library of Congress Cataloging-in-Publication Data
Library of Congress Catalog Card Number: 96-84751
ISBN 0-9652585-0-5


Gill Lui, Elizabeth
(1951–    )
SPIRIT AND FLIGHT, A Photographic Salute to the
United States Air Force Academy/Elizabeth Gill Lui
Place of Publication: USAF Academy, Colorado
Publisher: Association of Graduates of the United States Air Force Academy, 1996
160 pages: I-XXV, 1-135: col. ill.; 25.5cm
1. United States Air Force Academy-Pictorial  2. United States Air Force Academy--Buildings
3. United States Air Force Academy, Cadet Chapel. I. Title

Technical notes:
All photographs shot on Kodak Transparency Films, using either a Sinar 4x5, a Pentax 6x7 or a Leica R-3
Electronic files created in QuarkXpress™
Text set in Helvetica and Engravers Roman
Printing by Richtman's Printing on 80# Vintage Velvet Book by Potlach, Inc.
Englewood, Colorado
Binding by Roswell Bookbinding, Phoenix, Arizona


*NO PHOTOGRAPHIC IMAGES PRESENTED IN THIS PUBLICATION HAVE BEEN ELECTRONICALLY
ALTERED OR COMPUTER ENHANCED IN ANY MANNER WHATSOEVER.*

# CONTENTS

*Our national security, in a period of rapid change, will depend on constant reappraisal of our present doctrine, on alertness to new developments, on imagination and resourcefulness and new ideas. This is what we need for leadership in our military services, for the Air Force officer of today and tomorrow requires the broadest kind of scholarship to understand a most complex and changing world.*

JOHN F. KENNEDY

LOVINGLY DEDICATED

TO THE MEMORY

OF

MISS ATHA MOORMAN

1912–1990

To Begin

*Your attendance at the Academy has prepared you to enter the military profession by providing you core values. You've read them, seen them, heard them. They include striving for excellence in all that you do; putting service above self; and understanding that integrity, at the personal and institutional level, is the glue that binds the Force together.*

*Duty, honor, integrity...they define what we are and what we will be.*

GENERAL RONALD R. FOGLEMAN

SERVICE BEFORE SELF

INTEGRITY
FIRST

EXCELLENCE
IN ALL WE DO

# ARTIST'S PREFACE AND ACKNOWLEDGEMENTS BY ELIZABETH GILL LUI

The beauty of the Air Force Academy captured my imagination in the early 1960s when I moved with my family to Colorado Springs. As a dependent in an Air Force family I made many visits to the Academy, for church, for Sunday brunch, for football games with the requisite tailgate picnics, for various musical performances at Arnold Hall, and of course visits to view the wonder of the Universe at the Planetarium. Childhood memories of this kind are indelible, and I believe that my love of a modernist aesthetic in architecture can probably be traced back to these early impressions. My experience of the Academy superimposed in my mind the magnificent beauty of a Colorado landscape with the order and excellence of the architectural design of a university dedicated to learning and leadership.

Modernism, as a style in architecture, has characterized much of the look of our century with its attempt to combine the intricacies of engineering and industry with the aesthetics of geometry and an intellectual order. The Academy is one of the extremely exceptional examples of the international style of modernism, and is especially unique because of its isolated site within a natural environment. In urban areas buildings are influenced by their juxtaposition with other buildings that may differ in style, and therefore alter our impressions of them. A wonderful aspect of the

Academy is the bold and beautiful contrast between the great magnificence of nature and the geometric design of the human mind that is manifested in the architecture. Nature and architecture come together at the Academy in a profound combination of natural and human creativity. It is amidst an environment as elegant and excellent as the Academy that we are inspired as human beings to be the best that we can be. Such is the sentiment expressed by Winston Churchill when he said, "first we shape our architecture, thereafter it shapes us."

I was honored in 1986 with a commission by the Association of Graduates to create a photographic portrait of the Academy, with a primary focus on its architecture and environment. The images created at that time hung for five years in the Visitor's Center, finding their permanent home in Doolittle Hall in 1992. From the inception of this project it had always been envisioned that the photographs would be published as a book, celebrating and honoring the visual legacy of the Academy. *Spirit and Flight* is thus the culmination of this vision, and would never have been possible without the sustained commitment of the Association of Graduates to its publication.

My hope for this volume has been to capture both the spirit of what the architectural designers of the Academy originally envisioned it to be, and even more importantly the spirit of what it has become in the years it has existed in the world of humanly created things. Great Architecture, like all great Art, is enriched and transformed by the power of time and human experience, and not unlike many renowned monuments, the Air Force Academy transcended controversy to become one of our nation's most cherished architectural treasures.

My indebted thanks goes first to Lieutenant Colonel (Retired) Richard M. Coppock, the President and CEO of the AOG since 1983, who has been supportive of my work from the very beginning. His patience and perseverance throughout the many stages of this project have sustained both me and the work, and to him goes much of the credit for its successful actualization. The invaluable assistance, practical input, and moral support from his vice president, Colonel (Retired) Jock Schwank, has helped refine many of the details of a project of this scope, and it is to both of them as worthy collaborators that I extend my heartfelt appreciation.

Many years have passed since I made my first photos of the Academy, but I remember fondly the enthusiastic support I received from (then) Colonel Randy Cubero. (Now that he is a Brigadier General, I can tell how long it really has been!) It was with Randy as my escort that I photographed the Cadet areas closed off the the public, the falcon mews, and with whom I soared heavenward in my one and only flight in a sailplane. His invisible presence exists in many of these images and I thank him for his help and some very special memories.

As the project neared completion I gained incredible insight into Academy history from Donald J. Barrett, Librarian of the renowned Gimbel Historical Aeronautics Library, and it is courtesy of him that the book is enhanced with fascinating details of Academy 'trivia'. His 41 year tenure at the Academy makes him the longest tenured civilian employee, and with his seemingly limitless knowledge of Academy history he has been, and certainly not only for me, an inspiring resource.

The eloquent introduction by General Malham Wakin that follows is an addition to this work for which I am deeply appreciative. His words and works have influenced countless Academy students and contributed profoundly to the personal attainment of excellence for which so many of this fine institution's graduates are renowned. On a personal note, but one I know would be echoed by many, I am grateful to him for the integrity of his scholarship on the truly profound issues of war and morality. His authoritative anthology, *War, Morality and the Military Profession* is thought provoking and inspiring while soberly and humanistically addressing some of the most serious issues of our times, complex issues which clearly deserve passionate public dialogue. I am honored and grateful that he consented to share his thoughts with us on the occasion of this publication.

I would most like to thank my dear friend Walter A. Netsch, not only for his friendship, his support of my work, and his direct contributions to this book, but even more for the beautiful gift of an enduring architecture which he has given to all humanity. The Academy Chapel, an acknowledged masterwork of this century, has inspired moments of transcendence and awe in countless imaginations. In the true spirit of excellence to which the Academy is dedicated we have all benefited from the vision and contribution of Walter's commitment to the best within himself. I am honored to know him and forever grateful for his humanity and creative vision.

My dedication of this book to Miss Atha Moorman, wife of Academy superintendent (1965–1970) Lieutenant General Thomas S. Moorman, is deeply rooted in my respect for Miss Atha as a visionary woman whose contributions to the quality of excellence at the Academy and the Colorado Springs community is well respected within the Academy family. As a lifelong family friend Miss Atha always impressed me with her love of the arts and her commitment to her community. She was influential in bringing the study of the arts and the humanities to the Academy, as she believed in the need for Air Force leaders to be well rounded in their education. Her grace, dignity, and elegance are remembered lovingly by those who knew her, and I among them hope that the spirit of beauty captured in this volume pays honorable respect to her memory.

My sincerest gratitude is extended to my professional assistant Sherri Evans who has supported not only this project with her technical expertise, but perhaps even more invaluable supported me personally with her ever patient understanding, her humor and her emotional support. Her hand and heart are on every page of this book and I am more than grateful to have shared the journey with her.

I lastly thank my father, Colonel Richard M. Gill, 1918–1994, who showed me throughout his life and his career in the Air Force the deeply human side of the military. Through his example I came to appreciate the intrinsic honor and integrity of those men and women who have sacrificed in order to serve, and the ineffable value of the freedom that our country enjoys because of the unwavering commitment to duty that is at the core of a sustainable peace.

May this peace bless us always.

Elizabeth Gill Lui
Colorado, May 1996

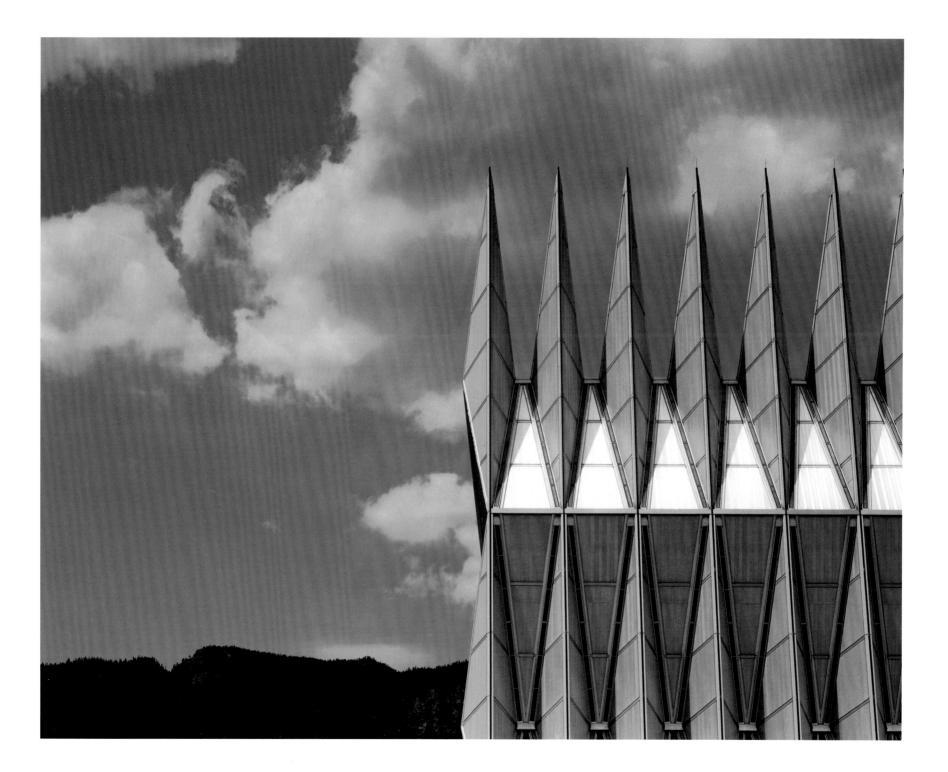

INTRODUCTION
BY
BRIGADIER GENERAL
MALHAM M. WAKIN
USAF (RETIRED)

In just a few years the Air Force Academy complex will have been in existence for fifty years and like its counterpart federal academies will undoubtedly be designated a national historical site. This will make it a very special place for the people of the United States who visit it in such large numbers, but in the hearts of those of us who have spent from four to forty years on these grounds there are more unique memories here – the stuff to evoke a nostalgic tear or two.

Aluminum and steel and glass and colored Italian mosaic tile – how different from the traditional old brick and ivy which characterized educational institutions in other parts of the country. Yet, how responsive and fitting this architecture has proven to be against the magnificent national backdrop of the Rampart Range of the Rockies. Modern? Yes and truly appropriate for the newly independent service branch. Many of us feel independent and proud and unafraid to be innovative in our approaches to curriculum and leadership and creative projects which this very environment challenges us to undertake. The first federal military academy to offer elective courses – the first to offer and then require academic majors – cooperative graduate programs – astronautics majors at the undergraduate level– accreditation before we even graduated our first class – gliders in the back yard – parachuting for fun! – flying as a competitive sport – athletic fields and facilities that almost demand our participation – who would dare not to strive for excellence in this magnificent place!

When the inspiring spires of the chapel rose to dominate the cadet area and mimic the majesty of the peaks beyond, there were those who excoriated us for our "blasphemy." How audacious of us to spend three million dollars for a church on a military installation and to make a house of worship such an overpowering presence. Could a good God support the purposes of an institution preparing leaders to make war? Yet, how much easier in the shadow of those spires has it been to remind ourselves of the proper use of the awesome weapons placed in our hands. How strongly we feel the trust that has been ours to constrain the use of force – to use it only for just causes with proper intentions and with proper proportion and discrimination. In the soft glow of the stained glass before the suggestive curves of the modern cross, one finds it remarkably appropriate to teach and adopt those core values of integrity first, service before self, and excellence in all we do.

The other buildings and monuments of the Academy conjure up memories for many: Vandenberg Hall and friendships formed; Fairchild Hall and lessons learned; favorite instructors and academic agony. Did we realize then that Fairchild Hall was one of the largest self-contained academic buildings in the world? With its extension in 1968 it housed faculty offices for 500-plus faculty members, laboratories and classrooms for 4,400 students, and the Academy library with its spectacular marble spiral staircase. The 1996 addition adjoining Fairchild Hall has remained true to the architectural design and, miraculously, fits beautifully into the landscape as though it had always been planned that way. When the new dormitory was built on the south side of the cadet quadrangle and later named for our medal of honor winner, Lance Sijan, it was as though that was the announcement of our maturity. One of our own had forever done us proud and Sijan Hall will keep fresh for many generations of cadets the ultimate mission of the Academy. And what graduate has not stood before the dark-faced graduate war memorial at the north end of the Air Gardens to shed a tear and murmur a prayer for a fellow-cadet who gave life itself in service to us all?

The cadet gym, Falcon Stadium, Eisenhower Golf Course, the field house, and Stillman Parade Field all carry memories of striving and sweat, victories and disappointments, dress uniforms and flybys – all contributing to the growth into the persons we hoped to be. And Mitchell Hall which we marched or stumbled to everyday with its vast expanse of glass and the staff tower and high ceiling – did you know that the entire roof was raised all at once? Memories of graduation buffets shared with proud families and the military balls in Arnold Hall. Some of us will remember Arnold Hall for its social amenities and some will even remember the "to be endured" evening lectures by famous and not-so-famous heroes, politicians, and scholars.

There is a special place, east of the cadet area and across the road from the golf course where many members of the Academy family rest forever. We lose our graduates earlier than most institutions because of the mission which justifies our existence. This commitment binds our community together as no Greek letter fraternity or other academic tradition ever could. The buildings and monuments of the Air Force Academy in their beautiful setting continue to reassure us that our commitment to country and to principle remains rock solid. Perhaps the magnificent artistry of Elizabeth Gill Lui displayed in this book will stir our hearts a bit and rekindle special memories.

Mal Wakin

## 1996 TWENTY-FIVE YEAR AWARD

IN RECOGNITION

OF THE

### UNITED STATES AIR FORCE ACADEMY
### CADET CHAPEL

AN OUTSTANDING COLLABORATION OF

DESIGN AND TECHNOLOGY,

THIS ICON OF CLEANLY ARTICULATED STRUCTURE

CONNECTS EARTH TO HEAVEN –

ITS SPECTACULAR ROCKY MOUNTAIN SURROUNDINGS

TO ITS ECCLESIASTICAL PURPOSE.

WITHIN THE CHAPEL, TOO, THE EYE IS DRAWN UPWARD,

NATURALLY, REVERENTLY.

ARTISTICALLY AHEAD OF ITS TIME,

THE CADET CHAPEL CONTINUES AND WILL CONTINUE

TO INSPIRE WORSHIP AND AWE.

*AMERICAN INSTITUTE OF ARCHITECTS*

Madam Secretary, Supreme Court Justice Stephen Breyer, Members of the Architectural Foundation, Officers and Members of the AIA and Guests.

This evening *Accent on Architecture 1996* is celebrating the Twenty-Five Year Award for the Air Force Academy Chapel.

I would like to go back to 1962 when Skidmore Owings & Merrill won its first firm award and the Chapel was the last building to be completed for the original corps size of 2,640 cadets.

To go back is to remind us of the character of modern architecture created then by SOM. For without the body of work this evening would not be; SOM would not have had the commission for the Academy and the overall design for the Academy. The Chapel in particular would not have happened without the principals in the firm at that time, and the design principles at that time, and the times themselves.

The victory of WWII was not on the battlefield alone. In our brilliance of invention, academic participation, industrial might and the overwhelming belief in a just cause, unbelievable impetus was given to all of us to make the needs of the post-war reflect the same enthusiasm.

In architecture and the arts the infusion of the emigres from Europe (Gropius, Neutra, Gideion, Aalto, Sert, Mendelsohn, Corbusier, Mies, et al) gave the aesthetic road map for American modern architecture and architectural education.

The designers in our group made interpretations of the modern movement as our education and beliefs possessed. We were all spurred on by Nat Owings who expected SOM to be the best.

The historian Henry Russell Hitchcock attributes the aesthetic results to, I quote, "Fortunately the looseness of the SOM organization, the importance of designers in its hierarchy, and the inclusion of engineers in the firm, have encouraged a greater degree of experimentation than might have been expected."

Needless to say this accent on design by the firm had its internal tumult and the Chapel was a prize example. Architectural change, as no other art form, is so interdependent on culture, on technology, on human response, and on designer dedication, and therefore so dependent on the times.

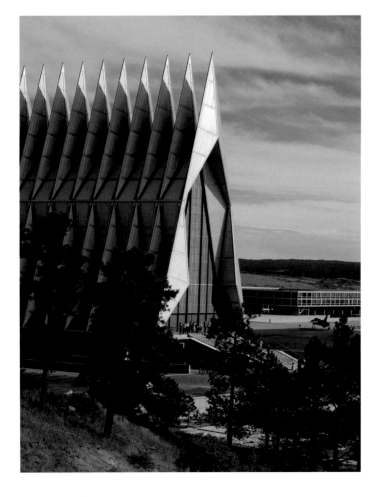

In the post WWII years the building industry was waiting, was hungry for new ideas and products, on extending the available but unused technology and we as designers were only too willing to participate. We saw this component as the American addition to the modern movement born in Europe.

My crisis then was not to try to duplicate the impossible, not just to recreate, but to invent in modern terms the third service academy place of worship. The design would not have happened without the character of the site, without the character of the buildings and site plan already under construction, without Dan Kiley's landscape and gardens, and without the support first and foremost of Nat Owings and Gordon Bunshaft, and then Eero Saarinen and Pietro Belluschi of the Air Force Secretary's Consultant Team.

But I must admit there would be no Chapel without the great defense by Secretary of the Air Force Douglas, by the benign support of Superintendent General Harmon, Senator Margaret Chase Smith serving on the Congressional review committee and the testimony of the American Institute of Architects.

The Chapel and the Academy was a major effort to define America's place in the modern movement. For me it was an end and a beginning, for with the Chapel began a new search in the redefinition in form, the expansion beyond the "box" and the further faith in geometry as the source of architectural form.

Thank you for this honor.

Walter Netsch

# A Photographic Salute
## To The
# United States Air Force Academy

# RECOLLECTIONS
## BY WALTER NETSCH

## MEMORY ONE

## THE LAND

It is a cool crisp morning
After a breakfast before sunrise
We take highway 85/87 to the flat land
On the highway opposite Lehman Mesa

And watch the sunrise on the
Rampart Range and follow the light down
The fingers of green
And wait to see
If the helicopter comes

We see the pines and scrub oak on the
South slope and the Douglas Firs
On the north and the range grass
In the valleys marked by cattle trails

The cattle don't pay attention anymore
But after our memory trip
We show a possible road alignment
To the pilot and sitting in the open
door of the helicopter
We ride our road

Over and over with eyes
With cameras
And thank the pilot and take
The jeep over the same route

Each day it gets better than ever

# CADET HYMN

**I**

Lord, guard and guide the men who fly
Through the great spaces of the sky;
Be with them traversing the air
In darkening storms or sunshine fair.

**II**

You who support with tender might
The balanced birds in all their flight,
Lord of the tempered winds, be near,
That, having you, they know no fear.

**III**

Control their minds with instinct fit
Whene'er, adventuring, they quit
The firm security of the land;
Grant steadfast eye and skillful hand.

**IV**

Aloft in solitude of space,
Uphold them with your saving grace.
O God, protect the men who fly
Through lonely ways beneath the sky.

Failures do not exist,
only varying degrees of success.

– Dewey Reinhard, 1984

# Memory Two

## The Site

Driving up Lehman Valley towards Lehman Mesa
The range looms larger and larger
We have our own small peak of craggy stone
To identify us from the highway

The land looks so flat
till we move just one hundred yards
and find we have dropped five feet.
The problems of infinity...
to build a piece of land
that airmen can form on and march on.

There must be walls and fill,
but to make the walls too high
will screen the campus
and make it look like a medieval fortress.

But the key came.
I thought of two up and two down
for the cadet quarters.
The building would be low in scale
on the campus,
and bold to the public,
becoming a retaining wall allowing us
to terrace the land.

The ramps, their slope define the scale.
Forest north and south,
then east and west,
then north and south again.
Joining terraces and structures with their needs...
All working together with the land.

The south slope of the mesa
becomes our link with nature.
The land we need for terraces of the campus
comes from the land we need
to build the flat playing fields,
thus Lehman Valley and Lehman Mesa
become the lands for the cadets.

The land is so rich and beautiful.
The valleys so contained.
Each have their own character...
We must do as little as possible to the land.

The mission of the Air Force Academy is to Develop and Inspire Air and Space Leaders with Vision for Tomorrow.

*Our current exploration of space is testimony to man's vision and to man's courage. The journey of the astronauts is more than a technical achievement; it is a reaching-out of the human spirit. It lifts our sights; it demonstrates that magnificent conceptions can be made real.*

*Our astronauts inspire us and at the same time they teach us true humility. What could bring home to us more the limitations of the human scale than the hauntingly beautiful picture of our earth seen from the moon?*

*When the first man stands on the moon next month, every American will stand taller because of what he has done, and we should be proud of this magnificent achievement.*

*We will know then that every man achieves his own greatness by reaching out beyond himself, and so it is with nations. When a nation believes in itself – as Athenians did in their golden age, as Italians did in the Renaissance – that nation can perform miracles. Only when a nation means something to itself can it mean something to others.*

*That is why I believe a resurgence of American idealism can bring about a modern miracle – and that modern miracle is a world order of peace and justice.*

RICHARD NIXON

The first graduate of the Academy on 3 June 1959 was Bradley C. Hosmer. He was also the Academy's first Rhodes Scholar.

Karol J. Bobko, Class of 1959, was the first Academy graduate to fly as an astronaut. He flew the maiden voyage of the space shuttle Challenger.

The only graduate to receive the Medal of Honor was Captain Lance P. Sijan, Class of 1965. He died while a Prisoner of War in North Vietnam on 22 January 1968.

The first 157 women joined the Cadet Wing on 28 June 1976 as members of the Class of 1980. 97 of them graduated on 28 May 1980. The first woman to serve as Wing Commander was Michelle D. Johnson, Class of 1981, who was Wing Commander for Spring 1981.

*Your choice, your choice, ladies and gentlemen, to take on the problems and possibilities of this time, to engage the world, not to run from it, is the right choice.*

*As you have learned here at the Academy, it demands sacrifice. In the years ahead, you will be asked to travel a long way from home, to be away from your loved ones for long stretches of time, to face dangers we perhaps cannot yet even imagine. These are the burdens you have willingly agreed to bear for your country, its safety, and its long-term security.*

*Go forth, knowing that the American people support you, that they admire your dedication. They are grateful for your service. They are counting on you to lead us into the 21st century, and they believe you truly do represent the best of America.*

*Good luck, and Godspeed.*

BILL CLINTON

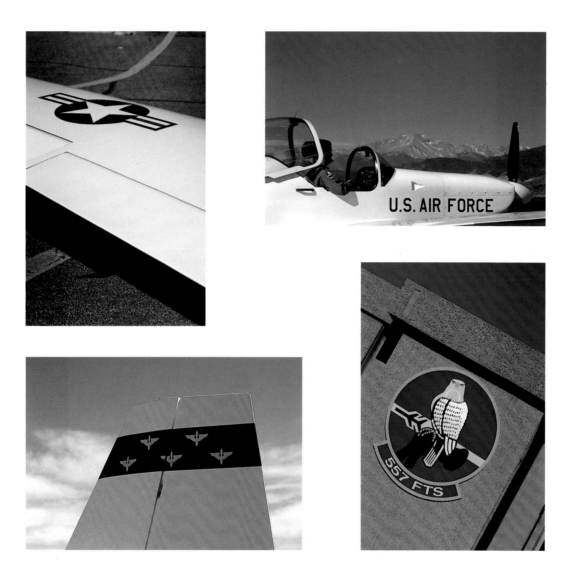

# THE FALCON

The noble falcon has long been an object of high esteem and pride for those fortunate enough to possess one of these magnificent birds. The falcon was so valued by early day nobility that they often restricted the possession of these birds to themselves. As early as 2000 B.C. falcons were used by Chinese nobles for hunting. Other records of falconry have been found in Japan, India, Iran, Arabia, Syria, and North Africa. In America the falcon has been used for centuries by the Navajo Indians as their symbol of war in the form of the Thunderbird.

In a dive, a falcon may attain speeds in excess of 200 miles per hour, but because its blood stream is not highly affected by gravitational pull, it can execute 180 degree turns at this high rate of speed in a fraction of a second – withstanding the resultant high "G" forces.

Because of their proud spirit, the training of falcons requires patience, careful attention, and gentle understanding. During the training period, the falcon is taught to associate mealtime with his trainer's whistle, so that the falconer, rather than the field quarry, is the center of the falcon's attention. The test of falcon and handler comes when the bird is taken out to an open field and released. The handler lifts his gloved fist and the falcon soars aloft, unrestrained by anything but the tenuous and precarious hold of training. After tasting the freedom of unlimited sky, the falcon returns to his master's fist.

The falcon fears neither man nor beast, and claims the world's atmosphere as its domain. This magnificent bird has been said to be the most highly developed and superlatively specialized flying organism on our planet, combining in a marvelous degree the highest powers of speed and aerial adroitness with massive, warlike strength. The falcon is the Air Force Cadet Wing mascot because this fearless, powerful, and extremely courageous bird typifies the spirit of the United States Air Force.

*Our willingness to accept the challenge of space will reflect whether America's men and women today have the same bold vision, the same courage and indomitable spirit that made us a great Nation. Where would we be if the brave men and women who built the West let the unknowns and dangers overwhelm them? Where would we be if our aviation pioneers let the difficulties and uncertainties sway them?*

*The only limits we have are those of our own courage and imagination. And our freedom and well-being will be tied to new achievements and pushing back new frontiers.*

RONALD REAGAN

# Memory Three

## The Process

In 1954 everything had to be hand drawn, the models painstakingly developed (hand planting 3,000 small brushes dyed green disguised as pines!) and developing a visual story for each of the areas, the master plan, the cadet areas, housing, and service and supply.

Today there is always a debate over how much time to spend on the computer and how much in models and drawings. But back then we did not even have patterned paper we could glue on, so that all our presentation drawings had hundreds of hand rendered prisma color lines.

Our basic drawing of the cadet area was about six feet square with all the contours drawn, with our landscape designer Dan Kiley's famous tree stamps hand applied in the tens of thousands. The drawing was so large it was intimate with the scale of our field view. We also had a 2x3 foot cardboard model in white of the U.S. geodetic survey so that we could get the feel of the site as a whole. There were finally over 60,000 drawings and sketches by the completion of the Academy!

After weeks of a grueling schedule and many sleepless nights the exhibit was a great success, except for the design for the chapel. I had thought it a disaster and hid in the back room in tears. Nat Owings, the project's manager for SOM, came over and said, "What's wrong with you? Everything has been approved but the chapel and you can always do another one."!

Several days later Nat came and asked if I had ever been to see Notre Dame in Paris. I reminded him I had been in the Aleutians during the war. Nat advised that I had better go to Europe for inspiration, that the next chapel design would meet with controversy and would probably be the focus of a congressional investigation. Unfortunately, he was right.

On the fields of friendly strife are sown the seeds
that on other days and other fields will bear the fruits of victory.

– General Douglas MacArthur

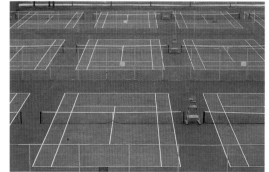

JACK'S VALLEY

The first Air Force freshman football game was against the University of Denver freshmen on 8 October 1955 at Denver University Stadium, won by Air Force 34-18.

The first varsity football game was played in 1956 against the University of San Diego in San Diego, and was won by Air Force 46-0.

The Academy's "home" football stadium was Denver University Stadium from 1955 through 1961. Games were also played at Penrose Stadium, now the site occupied by the Broadmoor West Hotel, at Washburn Field at Colorado College, at Pueblo Stadium, and Folsom Field at Boulder. Falcon Stadium was opened in 1962.

The Falcons only undefeated football team was the 1958 team with a 9-0-1 regular season record, and a 0-0 tie in the Cotton Bowl against Texas Christian University.

The first football game against Army was in 1959, a 13-13 tie played at Yankee Stadium in New York. The first victory over Army was 14-3 in 1965 at Soldier Field in Chicago.

The first football game against Navy was in 1960, a 35-3 loss played at Baltimore Memorial Stadium. The first victory over Navy was 15-7 in 1966 at Falcon Stadium.

*Through strength of example and commitment, we lead. You've been taught the price and the importance of leadership. As you leave the Academy, you answer your nation's call to advance the cause of freedom – to lead. There's a new sense of pride and patriotism in our land. And it's good for our nation's soul.*

*Patriotism binds the real and lasting fabric of our nation. Assertive but not arrogant – self-assured, kind, generous – we remain committed to our fundamental values.*

*So today I speak to you, and to every member of America's Armed Forces, to say thanks. When others weren't sure we were up to the task – you were. When your country asked you to serve – you did. And when others said, "No, no, we're not ready, we can't" – you said, "Yes. We are ready. We can." You and your colleagues in all the services prove that Americans consider no risk too great, no burden too onerous to defend our interests and our principles – in short, to do what's just and to do what's right.*

GEORGE BUSH

USAFA CADET HONOR GUARD
DRILL TEAM

*Let me say to this class, I know that the rewards of serving on the front lines of our foreign policy may seem distant and uncertain at times. Thirty-four years ago, President Kennedy said, "When there is a visible enemy to fight, the tide of patriotism runs high. But where there is a long, slow struggle with no immediate visible foe, your choice will seem hard indeed."*

*You should be very proud of what you have already accomplished. But you should be sobered by the important responsibilities you are about to assume. From this day forward, every day you must defend our Nation, protect the lives of the men and women under your command, and represent the best of America.*

The men and women of our Armed Forces remain the foundation, the fundamental foundation of our security. You put the steel into our diplomacy. You get the job done when all means short of force have been tried and failed.

All over the world, you have met your responsibilities with skill and professionalism, keeping peace, making peace, saving lives, protecting American interests. In turn, your country has a responsibility to make sure you have the resources, the flexibility, the tools you need to do the job. We have sought to make good on that obligation by crafting a defense strategy for our time.

BILL CLINTON

You may have to fight when there is no hope of victory,
because it is better to perish than to live as slaves.

– Sir Winston Churchill

*As you were commissioned you took an oath; an oath that focused on the Constitution and the nation. They are what we serve – not an individual, not an administration – but the United States of America, its citizens, and its democratic institutions...all symbolized by the Constitution.*

*By taking the oath of office, you have also agreed to live your lives under an "Unlimited Liability Clause." That is, if called upon to do so, you are expected to lay down your lives for your country, for your fellow Americans, for your families. No other profession demands such a commitment from its practitioners, but ours does. It's something we all live with as an accepted part of our day to day activities...whether in peacetime, crisis, or war.*

*And because we ask people to make the commitment to go in harm's way – to be prepared to make the ultimate sacrifice – we must have extraordinary leaders throughout our military services. You should aspire to become one of those leaders.*

GENERAL RONALD R. FOGLEMAN

Harmon Hall, the administrative center of the Academy, houses the offices of the superintendent and his staff. It was named in tribute to Lt. General Hubert R. Harmon, who worked from 1949 until 1954 on plans for an Air Force Academy, was instrumental in getting Congressional approval for the Academy, and was the Academy's first superintendent.

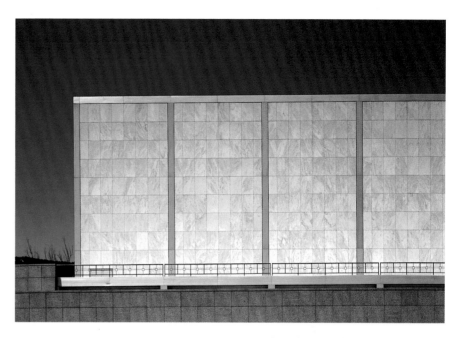

Arnold Hall was named after the first General of the Air Force, Henry "Hap" Arnold. General Arnold was Commanding General of the Army Air Corps during World War II and fought vigorously for a separate Air Force.

ARNOLD HALL

*I believe that we must balance our need for survival as a nation with our need for survival as a people. Americans, soldiers and civilians, must remember that defense is not an end in itself – it is a way of holding fast to the deepest values known to civilized men.*

*And I believe this above all: that this nation shall continue to be a source of world leadership, a source of freedom's strength, in creating a just world order that will bring an end to war.*

RICHARD NIXON

Mitchell Hall is named for Brigadier General William "Billy" Mitchell, a leader in the Army Air Corps in World War I and the early 1920s.

*You know, I was tempted to ask General Scowcroft how he thought I was performing during the war, but I was afraid he'd say, "Fast, neat, average, friendly, good, good."*

GEORGE BUSH

Fairchild Hall is named for General Muir S. Fairchild, first commander of the Air University, and former Vice Chief of Staff of the Air Force. He was in charge of a 1948 board which studied plans for the Academy's curriculum.

My generation wants to be remembered, not as the generation that suffered in war, but as the generation that was tempered in its fire for a great purpose: to make the kind of peace that the next generation will be able to keep.

It is my deepest hope and my belief that each of you will be able to look back on your military career with pride, not because of the wars in which you have fought, but because of the peace and freedom which your service will make possible for America and the world.

RICHARD NIXON

# The Colonel Richard Gimbel Aeronautical Library

The Gimbel Library, which is housed in a secure and humidified area in the AFA Library, comprises an amazing array of items pertaining to the history of flight. Five-thousand-year-old seals carved from semi-precious stones and used to make clay tablets, and some of the first printed allusions to flying document man's earliest dreams of flight. There are drawings, rare commemorative medallions and many books about early experiments with wings, initial balloon ascents, first parachutes, kites, pyrotechnics, historic aviation flights, imaginary voyages in space, and primitive rockets which contribute to a kaleidoscope of the history of man's aeronautical triumphs. Early flight manuals, catalogs of aircraft equipment, and other materials relating to airships, military aviation, and air accidents record the technological progress and problems of modern aeronautics.

French and English editions predominate among the approximately 6,000 books in the Collection which encompasses more than fifteen languages. Many of the books, in addition to their aeronautical significance are bibliographic treasures because they are superb examples of fine book binding, printing, illustration, and typography. One of the many exciting and fascinating topics extensively covered in the Gimbel Collection is the idea of imaginary voyages in space. Autograph enthusiasts can scrutinize with great interest the more than 250 autographs, holographs, and inscriptions in the Collection.

The Gimbel Library is greatly enriched by approximately 3,000 prints, portraits, and views, and includes engravings, etchings, woodcuts, lithographs, and drawings in black-and-white and in color making a truly unique pictorial history of aeronautics.

With a total of more than 20,000 items, the Gimbel Library is a comprehensive record of aeronautical history.

*Courtesy of The Gimbel Library*

*We do not dictate the courses nations follow, but neither can we overlook the fact that our example reshapes the world. We can't right all wrongs – but neither can any nation lead as we can.*

*You graduates will find that no other combat force you encounter will have your skills, your technology or support. You'll find that in world leadership we have no challengers, but in our turbulent world, you will find no lack of challenges. And I know you are ready.*

*So to all of America's servicemen – all of them, wherever they may be – and all of America's servicewomen, I salute them – I salute you.*

GEORGE BUSH

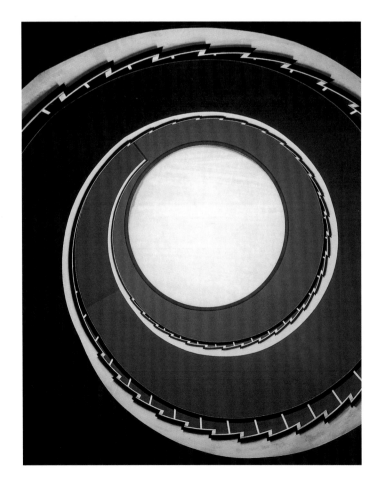

There are 93 steps in the spiral staircase in the Academic Library. There are two spiral stairs to the Arnold Hall Ballroom, two in the Arnold Hall Theater, one to the Mitchell Hall Staff Tower.

*By being on the ready, the Armed forces maintain the freedom, the security and the peace not only of the United States but of the dozens of countries who are allied to us.*

*This is the role which history and our own determination has placed upon a country which lived most of its history in isolation and neutrality and yet in the last 18 years has carried the burden for free people everywhere. I think that this is a burden which we accept willingly, recognizing that if this country does not accept it no people will. Recognizing that in the most difficult time in the whole life of freedom the United States is called upon to play its greatest role. This is a role which we are proud to accept and I am particularly proud to see the United States accept it in the presence of these young men who have committed themselves to the service of our country and to the cause of its freedom.*

JOHN KENNEDY

Sijan Hall was named in honor of Captain Lance P. Sijan, Class of 1965. He was the first Academy graduate to receive the Medal of Honor. Expansion of the Cadet Wing in 1964 to an authorized strength of 4,417 required the construction of additional dormitories. Construction of Sijan Hall began in 1965, and was completed in December 1967. It was known as the "New Dorm" until 31 May 1976 when it was dedicated in honor of Captain Sijan.

SIJAN HALL

CETF
CONSOLIDATED
EDUCATIONAL
TRAINING FACILITY

DEDICATION
AUGUST 1996

The true measure of a professional lies in his ability
to adapt to new situations.

— Honorable Harold Brown, Secretary of Air Force

USAFA HOSPITAL

Doolittle Hall, is the headquarters building and alumni house for the Association of Graduates. The facility is named in honor of the late General James H. "Jimmy" Doolittle. General Doolittle was awarded the Medal of Honor for his actions on April 18, 1942 when he voluntarily led 16 Army Air Force B-25s from the aircraft carrier Hornet on a daring low-level attack against Tokyo and the Japanese mainland.

The statue of Pegasus, the winged horse of Greek mythology, is a replica of the original at the Italian Air Force Academy in Florence, Italy. It was given to the Academy by the Italian Air Force in May 1959. It was relocated in March 1994 to the area in front of Doolittle Hall.

Duty then is the sublimest word
in the English language.
You should do your duty in all things.
You can never do more. You should never do less.

– General Robert E. Lee

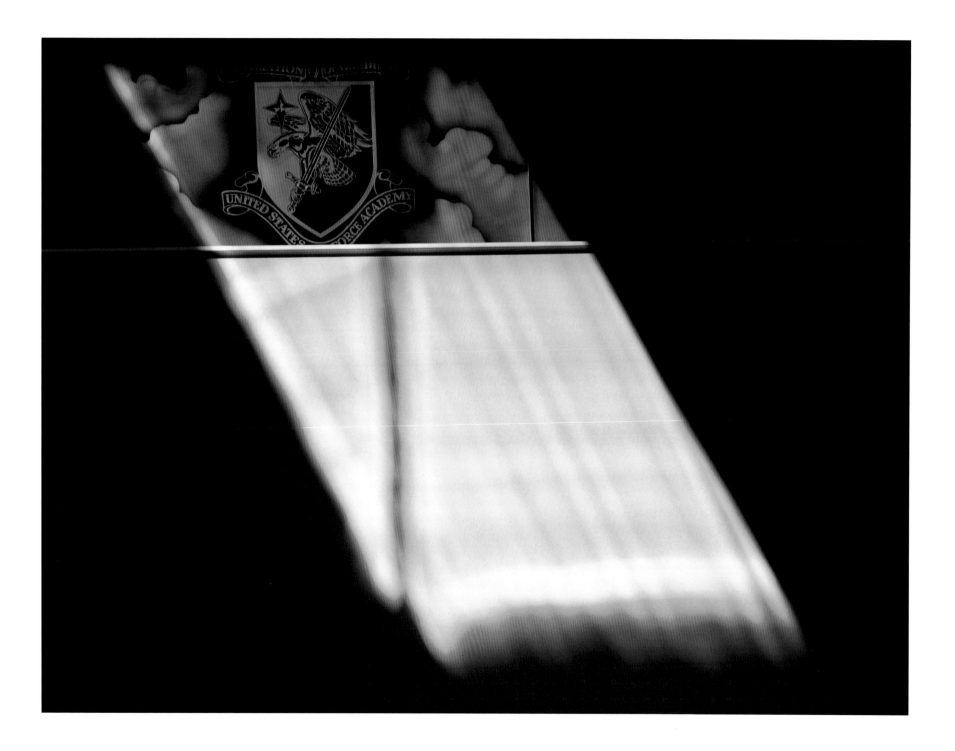

*Let your determination to make this world better and safer override all other considerations. This Academy was not built just to produce air warriors. It was also built to produce leaders who understand the great stakes involved in the defense of their country; leaders who can be entrusted with the responsibility to protect peace and freedom. You are those leaders. And while you must know better than those before you how to fight a war, you must also know better than those before you how to deter a war, how to preserve peace.*

RONALD REAGAN

# MEMORY FIVE

## AESTHETICS

Like every aesthetic movement modernism has certain attitudes, rather than rules. There are four that applied to the Air Force Academy.

The first was the use of PROPORTION. Falling back on my Japanese experience of the tatami oriented world the module of 7' x 7' was selected, and multiples or divisions of this proportion were used. This meant that within any structure system the solids and voids would relate.

The second was the use of SHADE. Shadow would be used to define form, and setbacks would provide the cadets covered walkways when they were not in formation.

The third was GEOMETRY, in that there was a relationship between the vertical and the horizontal. The ground plane corresponded to the vertical plane. This would contrast with nature's more complex character.

And the last was the use of COLOR. The buildings were to have a dignified, basic, quiet color, and then most importantly to make this work there would be accent colors. The Bauhaus colors of basic red, blue and yellow were the one sort of rule at the time, and it was from this that the colors of the mosaic walls were derived.

The small pieces of colored ceramic, called tesserae, were selected from Venetian mosaics for their fine size, elegant color match ability, and most importantly for their texture. As these small bits vary in thickness they give a wonderful texture that gives sparkle to the broad colored wall surfaces on which they are applied.

I guess many people like them as souvenirs for they try to dig them out of the walls of Harmon Hall. Don't do that-it doesn't look good, it's bad manners, and it's darn hard to replace each little ceramic!

*Personal honor, courage, and professional competence will guide your thoughts and actions. You understand the horrors of war, and you know that peace with freedom is the highest aspiration of our time.*

*The greatest privilege of my office has been to lead the people who defend our freedom and whose dedication, valor and skill increase so much our chance to live in a world of peace...*

*Your experience at this magnificent institution – guided by honesty, integrity, and an abiding loyalty to our Nation – will serve you well.*

RONALD REAGAN

## HONOR OATH

We will not lie, steal, or cheat, nor tolerate among us anyone who does. Furthermore, I resolve to do my duty and live honorably, so help me God.

The plaques on the Chapel wall feature the crests of the USAFA graduating classes. The center position on the wall is occupied by the crest of the current year's senior class.

Today air power is the dominant factor in war. It may not win a war by itself alone, but without it no major war could be won.

– Arthur Radford, 1954

The Eagle and Fledglings statue in front of Mitchell Hall was presented by the Air Training Command in December 1958. The inscription "Man's flight through life is sustained by the power of his knowledge" was authored by Lt. Colonel Austin Miller.

MAN'S FLIGHT
THROUGH LIFE IS
SUSTAINED BY THE
POWER OF HIS
KNOWLEDGE.

*While our leaders are still defining America's role in a dramatically different post-Cold War world, it is clear that we stand alone as the world's superpower....With that recognition comes an awesome responsibility.*

*The United States of America is a great nation. It is a beacon of freedom and opportunity for all the world. But I and the other graduates who have gone before you have learned that freedom is not free.*

*On a monument on the terrazzo at the north end of the air gardens are the names of 157 graduates who have died in combat. The price of freedom is sacrifice and eternal vigilance. And by virtue of the profession you have chosen, the burden of that sacrifice and vigilance will fall on your shoulders.*

GENERAL RONALD R. FOGLEMAN

# Bring Me Men

## by Sam Walter Foss
## July 4, 1895

Bring me men to match my mountains,
Bring me men to match my plains;
Men to chart a starry empire,
Men to make celestial claims.
Bring me men to match my prairies,
Men to match my inland seas;
Men to sail beyond my oceans,
Reaching for the galaxies.
These are men to build a nation,
Join the mountains to the sky;
Men of faith and inspiration,
Bring me men, bring me men, bring me men!
Bring me men to match my forests,
Bring me men to match my shore;
Men to guard the mighty ramparts,
Men to stand at freedom's door.
Bring me men to match my mountains,
Men to match their majesty;
Men to climb beyond their summits,
Searching for their destiny.
These are men to build a nation,
Join the mountains to the sky,
Men of faith and inspiration,
Bring me men, bring me men, bring me men!

As Published in Contrails 1992-1993

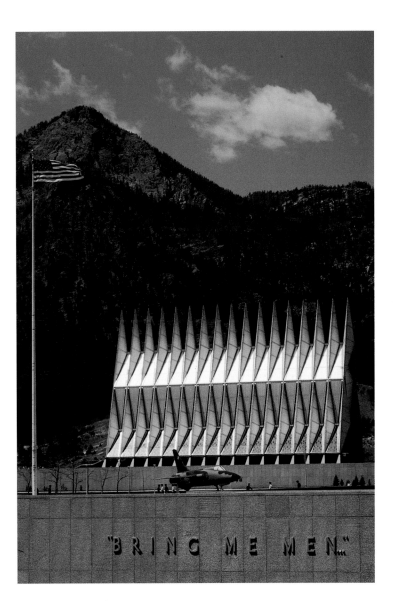

The power of excellence is overwhelming.
It is always in demand and nobody cares about its color.

– General Daniel "Chappie" James, 1972

*Clearly, the 21st century will be the century of air and space power. Much as the Roman Age was defined by the Legions which conquered the then-known world; and the European Age of Discovery and Exploration was dominated by great naval fleets that secured trade and commerce well into the modern era; the 21st Century will be known as the age of air and space power. Air power in the hands of democratic nations will be used to help provide humanitarian assistance, deter aggression, and secure peace.*

GENERAL RONALD R. FOGLEMAN

# Memory Six

## The Chapel

When I was told I had to redesign the chapel I first had to get all the buildings the cadets would need to use in the works, then I could take that trip to Europe, and then redesign the chapel.

The site of the chapel had become an issue. The chapel moved down the hill slowly, which had been thought to be too dominant and too separate from the cadets. It was out at the honor court, then far to the south into the trees that were there before Sijan, and then finally on the chapel's own island where it is now.

Everyone agreed that this was proper, including our SOM team and our consultants Eero Saarinen and Pietro Belluschi. With this site chosen, all that was needed was the building.

Finally with the location settled the chapel design was the priority. Remembering my trip to Europe I was seeking an appropriate form that would have a three dimensional character like a gothic cathedral. *The stone was the structure, the stone was the decoration, the stone was the pattern, the stone was the form.*

I would sketch on anything; my napkins at meals, a match box, the back of a bill. One day lunching with my engineer I was scribbling away and suddenly he asked, "Do you know what you are drawing? Those are tetrahedrons."

And then I began drawing in earnest, for the tetrahedrons were the three dimensional form I was seeking – *structure, shape, decoration.* But there was no glass, no luminosity. The idea came to me to separate the tetrahedrons creating a ribbon of colored light between them. The idea took form as a small section of interconnected tetrahedrons with spaces allowing for the radiance and clarity of colored light. Remembering earlier struggles and failures I was gratified with the approval that came from my colleagues, and I moved on to drawings for a whole building.

The final design of course changed to aluminum, as stone was out of the question – too heavy, too costly, probably too fragile, and at odds with my goals of holistic form. So the design developed and was modified, from 19 spires to 17, the use of the antiphonal choir, and eventually the window design. With support from the critical players, including the secretary of the Air Force and Academy representatives, the final basic design decision was made.

*Our progress results from human creativity and the opportunity to put our knowledge to use to make life better...*

*The greatest of all resources is the human mind. All other resources are discovered only through creative human intelligence. God has given us the ability to make something from nothing. And in a vibrant, open political economy, the human mind is free to dream, create, and perfect. Technology plus freedom equals opportunity and progress...*

*You should be confident that, with wisdom, responsibility, and care, you can harness change to shape your future.*

*We've only seen the beginning of what a free and courageous people can do. The bold, not the naysayers, will point the way, because history has shown that progress often takes its greatest strides where brave people transform an idea, which is scoffed at by skeptics, into a tangible and important part of everyday life.*

RONALD REAGAN

The cadet chapel was not built during the original construction of the Academy due to architectural controversy. It was begun on 28 August 1959, and was dedicated on 22 September 1963. The chapel is 150' high, 224' long, and 56' wide. It has seventeen spires. The inside height of the Protestant nave is 90'. The principal designer was Walter Netsch of Skidmore, Owings and Merrill.

JEWISH CHAPEL

CATHOLIC CHAPEL

# Memory Seven

## The Glass

The decision was approved to give a grotto character to the Catholic Chapel, a circle to the Jewish Chapel to represent the tent, and the primary form enclosing all the chapels to the Protestant Chapel. The glass design was still ahead as Gordon Bunshaft and I continued to draw inspiration from St. Chapelle and the Chapel of St. Francis in Assisi.

One winter I spent the evenings using colored pencils and colored over 10,000 spots to distribute the colored glass, and in the chapel you can see the results. The colors change from darker blues to reds to gold as the altar is approached and at the junctions of the tetrahedrons star bursts occur. The idea was formed.

With my research staff we hit upon the way of fracturing a thick irregularly shaped piece of glass to be used in this application. This would facet the glass, thereby bringing out it's brilliance. By randomly hitting the glass with a hammer anyone, even you or I, could achieve this medieval goal.

The pews and altars were special donations in all of the chapels. The Jewish Chapel was adorned with purple glass and stone for the flooring brought from Israel. The glass for the Catholic Chapel was designed to enhance the magnificent Stations of the Cross. The organ designer and I selected the location of various organ elements to fit the Protestant Chapel form.

With both idea and method in hand the glass would become the reality that would bathe each chapel with the inspiring power of Light.

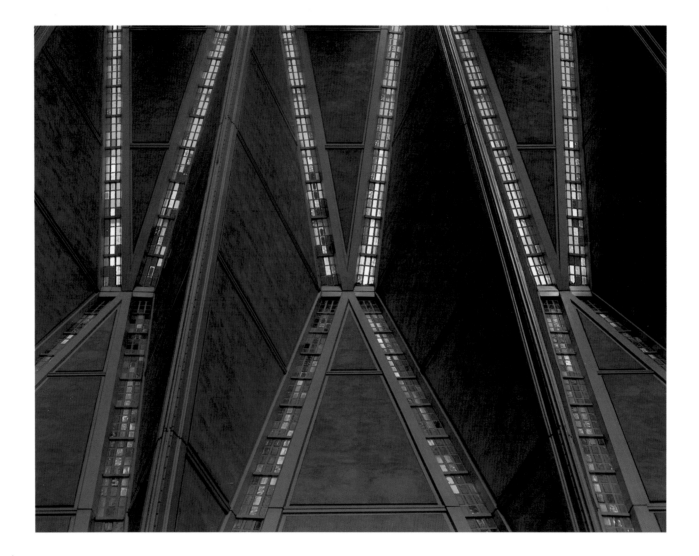

Integrity is the fundamental premise of military service in a free society. Without integrity, the moral pillars of our military strength, public trust and self respect are lost.

– General Charles A. Gabriel, Chief of Staff, 1985

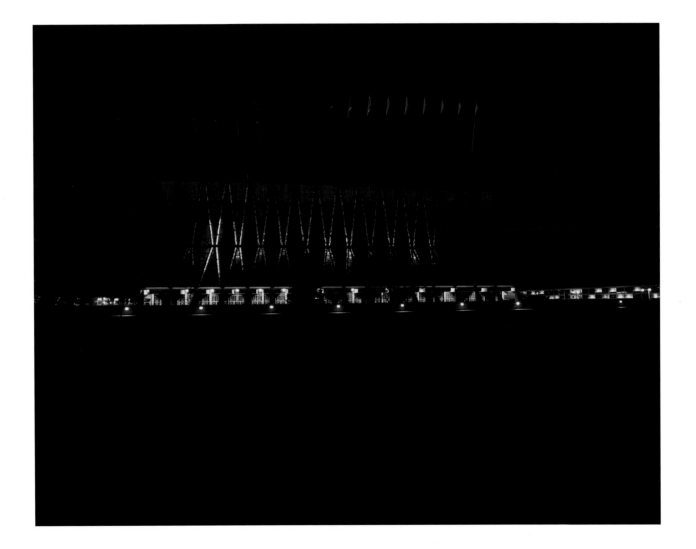

# IN CLOSING

## ELIZABETH GILL LUI

Elizabeth Gill Lui is a 1973 Phi Beta Kappa graduate of The Colorado College with a degree in comparative religion. She pursued graduate work at The Colorado College, the University of Denver, and the Graduate School of Design at Harvard University. Her international exhibition career in photography has taken her work to venues throughout the United States, France, the previous Soviet Union, Japan and Hong Kong. Her work emphasizes the aesthetics of mathematics and geometry in architecture and the natural world.

## Time line and basic data for the United States Air Force Academy

**1954**
- Skidmore, Owings and Merrill awarded contract
- Architectural team organized
- Academy design program finalized

**1955**
- Conceptual master plan approved
- Cadet area designs approved
- Exhibition of design proposal at the Colorado Springs Fine Art Center
- Controversy over Chapel design
- Master plan submitted
- Basic roads, utilities, and cadet area site grading begun
- SOM directed to relocate chapel

**1956**
- Dan Kiley design of Air Gardens approved
- Final Chapel site approved

**1957**
- Revised Chapel design concept presented and reviewed

**1958**
- Models for Cadet Area finalized
- Cadet buildings 90% complete
- Cadets begin occupancy
- Continued review of Chapel Design
- Approval for Academy road system
- Approval of Capehart Housing Area in association with KC Architects

**1959**
- First graduation

**1963**
- Chapel dedicated

## Academy Construction and Design Data

- 6,000 construction workers
- 52 contractors
- 2,500,000 cubic yards of earth used in reconfiguring mesa and terrace
- 2 miles of retaining walls
- Cadet dormitories covering 1/4 mile and 4 acres
- 32 miles of paved road
- 6 bridges

- 60,000 drawings & sketches
- 6,000 working drawings

...later in this ceremony as you throw your hats in the sky, and the Thunderbirds fly over, I ask that you take one last opportunity to embrace one another as classmates, to savor the moment of your success, and to celebrate the richness of your futures. And remember that while the defense of the Nation is a serious undertaking, you need not be serious all the time. Take the time to enjoy life and all the blessings that come from being an American.

GENERAL RONALD R. FOGLEMAN

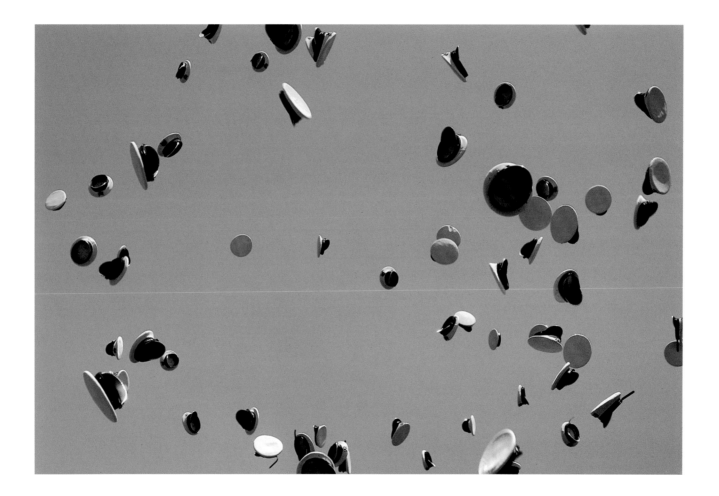

IN OUR HEARTS AND MEMORIES
THE ACADEMY REMAINS WITH US ALWAYS
GUIDING US AND REMINDING US
THAT HERE WE PASSED
FROM YOUTH TO MATURITY
FROM DISCIPLINE TO SERVICE
FROM DREAMS TO RESPONSIBILITY

WE FOREVER SALUTE
THE UNIQUELY BEAUTIFUL PLACE
WHERE THE JOURNEY
INTO OUR LIVES
BEGAN.

*ELIZABETH GILL LUI*